Listen

...What do you hear?

Library of Congress Cataloging-in-Publication Data

Wood, Nicholas, (date)
   Listen...what do you hear? / Nicholas Wood and Jennifer Rye;
illustrated by Julie Douglas.
      p.   cm.—(First science)
   Summary: Discusses the phenomenon of sound, how it varies in
volume and pitch, how it travels, and how it is perceived by the
ear.
   ISBN 0-8167-2120-3 (lib. bdg.)   ISBN 0-8167-2121-1 (pbk.)
   1. Sound-waves—Juvenile literature.   [1. Sound.] I. Rye,
Jennifer.   II. Douglas, Julie, ill.   III. Title.
QC243.2.W66 1991
534—dc20   90-40136

Published by Troll Associates, Mahwah, New Jersey 07430

Printed in the U.S.A.

10 9 8 7 6 5 4 3 2 1

Listen
...What do you hear?

Written by
Nicholas Wood
and Jennifer Rye

Illustrated by
Julie Douglas

Troll Associates

Close your eyes and listen.
What can you hear?
Water dripping from a faucet?
A fly buzzing?
Keep very still, and you can
even hear yourself breathing.

There are footsteps on the stairs.
The floorboards creak,
then the hinge squeaks
and the door opens.
Someone's coming in.
Who is it?
Look and see...

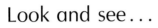

It's not a person at all!
He's listening, too.
He's hoping someone will say "walk."

Animals and people use their ears
to listen for sounds.
That is one way of finding out
what is going on around us.

Some sounds go on all the time,
like the ticking of a clock.
We get so used to them
that we stop noticing them.

When you drop a stone into water,
ripples spread out in waves.
Sounds travel in waves, too.
Only sound waves are invisible,
and can travel through the air.
You can't see them,
you can only hear them.

When sound waves reach your ear,
the skin inside vibrates like a drum.
Your brain understands
what the vibration means.

Sounds can be LOUD or soft.
They can be high or low.
Your brain has to make sense
of the sounds.

Sounds travel through air
at about 745 miles per hour.
Some jets go faster than that.
So watch out! If a jet
is flying overhead at full speed,
you may not hear it coming.

After it has gone past,
you will hear the roar of its engines.
The plane is moving faster
than its own noise!

Sounds that are near us can be loud.
Sounds further away will be quieter.
The sound gets quieter as it travels,
because the sound waves spread out.
If you want the sound to go further,
you have to help it along.
You can make a funnel with your hands
to collect the sound waves,
or you can use a bullhorn.

Try rolling up a piece of paper
and making a funnel with it.
Then talk to your friends through it.
They will be able to hear you
from a long way away.
Use the funnel to collect sound waves
when they reply.

Some people are deaf.
They may be able to hear a little,
or nothing at all.
Deaf people sometimes wear hearing aids
to make sounds louder.

Some deaf people learn
to read lips. They can see
what you are saying
by watching your lips move.

Some deaf people also use
a different language to talk.
They make signs with their hands
instead of noises with their mouths.

Words are sounds, too.
Babies cannot talk at first.
They can only cry.
They learn to talk by copying
the sounds that other people make.

They find out that different sounds
mean different things.
When we talk, our tongues
and our lips turn noises
into words. Try saying "bottle"
without moving your lips.
You need your lips and your tongue
to make words.

Ring...ring...ring...
What's that?
When the telephone rings,
someone wants to talk to you.
The telephone changes your voice
so it can travel along wires
like electricity.

You can talk to someone
in another house, another city,
or even another country.
If you are deaf, you can
have a telephone which
makes voices louder.

Sounds can be high-pitched,
like a whistle,
or low-pitched, like a cow mooing.
Humans can hear a range
of sounds from high to low.

Some animals can hear
much higher sounds than we can,
and much lower ones, too.
For example, dogs and cats
hear more than we do.
Some dog whistles make
high-pitched sounds that
people can't hear.
But a dog can!

Bats can make and hear
very high-pitched sounds.
As they fly around,
they click all the time.
The clicks bounce off things
that get in the way of the sound waves.

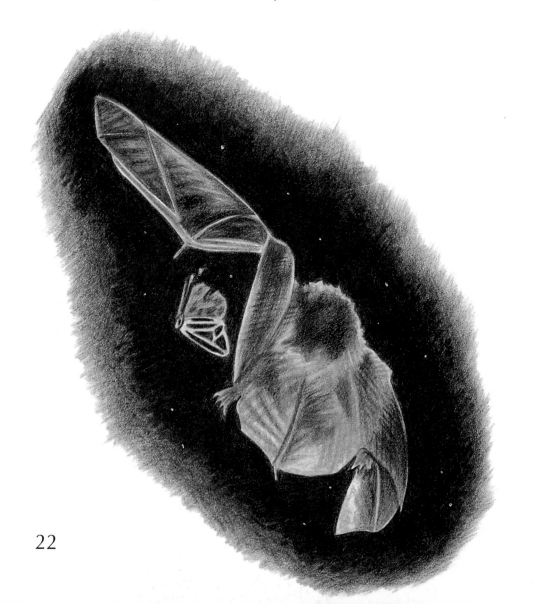

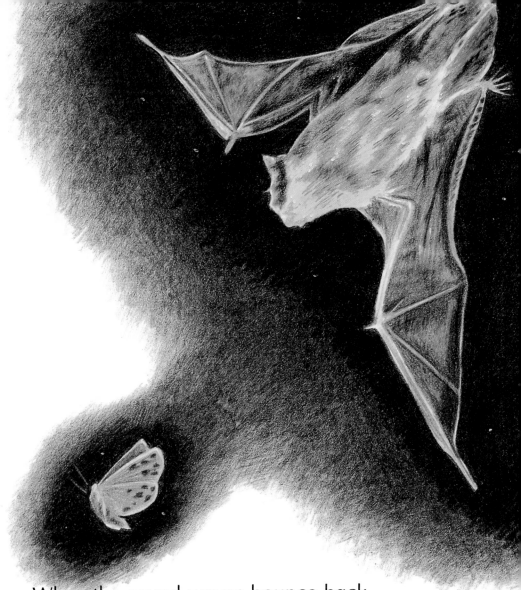

When the sound waves bounce back,
the bats hear an echo.
The echo warns them
that they may need to change direction.
They use these echoes to help them
find food and get around safely.

The echo system that bats use
is just like the sonar system
of a submarine.
The submarine sends sound waves
out into the water.
The sound waves bounce off
things that are deep in the sea.
Then the crew on the submarine
listens for the echoes.
That's how submarines get around
safely in the deep dark ocean
without bumping into things.

Boats on the surface also use sonar
when it is too foggy
or too dark to see.

Sounds travel a long way under water.
Whales call to each other
with their own songs,
which travel many miles
under the waves.

Animals need to hear
for different reasons.
Owls use their ears
to help them hunt.
They can hear very faint noises
that tell them where a mouse is hiding,
even though they can't see it.

Moths use their ears to help them escape
from bats that want to eat them.

Frogs make a noise
to tell other frogs where they are,
or to warn others to stay away
from that part of the pond.

We use sounds as warnings, too.
A fire alarm rings
when a building is on fire.
It warns everyone to go outside.
Burglar alarms and car alarms
warn of break-ins.
Police cars and ambulances
make a loud noise
to warn other drivers
to keep out of their way.

Car drivers blow their horns
and cyclists ring their bells.
When you cross the road,
you must listen for traffic
as well as looking
to see if it's safe.

Some noises are so loud
they can hurt our ears.
People who work
with noisy machines
sometimes wear earmuffs
to protect their eardrums.
Look at this man
digging a hole in the road.
He can still hear his drill,
but the noise is muffled.
He can't hear the dog
barking, though.

Giant radio telescopes
are like big ears that are
listening all the time
for sounds from space.
Perhaps, somewhere in space,
other people are trying to talk to us
or are listening to our world.

Sounds help animals and people
communicate and talk to each other.
Making and listening to sounds
helps us learn about
the world we live in.